A Flipped School

"Sometimes our greatest solutions have come from the most unlikely places!"

This book is dedicated to those who believed in us and to those who didn't. Both were our motivation and inspiration.

Forward

You ask me why I am an unabashed supporter of Clintondale High School?

Their names are Dana, Sarah, Cameron, Mary and Lizzie.

I live 50 miles from Detroit and Greg's school. Yet, I would travel every week (and sometimes multiple times) to take part in Clintondale's transformation.

You see, my five kids' school system is supposedly "better off," nestled next to fine Big 10 University. After school, my kids would have their varied after school activities, eat dinner, goof off and then settle down to homework.

My son, Cameron, would attempt his freshman Math homework. He'd look to his older sister for help. Sarah understood it. She "just gets" Math. Unfortunately, she can't explain it very well. So, my son's frustration with not being able to do his homework -- "I understood it in class" -- coupled with his sister's frustration that her brother doesn't get her explanations -- yielded more than a few tears.

You know the worst part? I thought it was Cameron's fault.

He should take better notes. He should take more responsibility for his learning. He should never leave class w/o a perfect understanding of the material. He should prepare better for class. Don't get me wrong. There's truth in all of these statements.

But, the truth is... the system is BROKEN.

And Greg has the temerity to speak the truth. I know it embarrasses a lot of educators because someone is saying, "Ah... Prince... You're butt naked!"

And, it's the truth!

Pop Quiz for the Non-Rocket Scientist: How long would you send your child to a sports coach who every Tuesday and Thursday afternoon talked about and demonstrated proper technique and sent your child home to practice on their own, asking them to show up for games "ready" to play?

You *might* give the coach a couple of weeks to see if this crazy approach would pan out. And if it did pan out, you'd be pretty sure it was because of the raw talent of some of the kids or extraordinary effort on the part of the kids. Bluntly: the kids would be succeeding despite the system.

Please do not get me wrong. I love and appreciate almost every one of my kids teachers. They almost universally put their heart and soul and bank accounts into their works. Incredibly long nights and weekends, trying to make class fun and engaging for their students. I support them and honor them for their work.

But to send a kid home to struggle alone is like asking water to flow uphill. Water will find the shortest path downhill. I believe that Clintondale has found the path that leads to less resistance and greater success.

I continue to be AMAZED at the work -- the HARD WORK -- of Clintondale High School students and teachers. They have adapted and excelled in what is a Grand Experiment!

Is it perfect? Heck NO! Can it be improved? They are trying everyday to learn and adapt to spend more time with the kids in class and let the kids practice when the coach/teacher is around.

My company played a small hand in setting up their computers and software that allowed them to flip. But, we simply planted some new grass on their field of play and they are playing one heck of a game. They are changing the rules of education. Changing what's expected. They are changing the results and literally changing the trajectory of the lives of the kids who grow up in one of America's most challenged cities.

Why do I support Greg Green and Clintondale? Because I am selfish. And I want that change to cross the globe and come home to nest in my town and bless the lives of my kids. And hopefully yours.

May you be as inspired by their story as I and my family have been.

Troy Stein
TechSmith Corporation

The first time I met Greg, he was visiting our offices at TechSmith to share his story with some of our Education team members. I was in the Public Relations team at that point, focusing on Education's use of technology in the classroom.

Greg shows up and starts telling us about how he has started a pilot project around flipping one of his 9th grade classes, then the whole 9th grade, and next the whole school. The PR side of my brain is spinning with possibilities on how to share his story out to other educators. But that same side of my brain is also thinking 'this sounds too good to be true. These results are beyond amazing. Too amazing. I need proof. I need to see the data.'

So I peppered Greg with question after question about his process, student & teacher reactions, challenges they ran into, training his staff to prepare them for this shift in educating, do his students have technology access outside of school walls... my questions were pretty endless. Greg was more than patient with my grilling, answered all of my questions and shared the data with me.

Once I saw the data his school had collected around failure rates and discipline rates improving drastically, I was floored. How did his school get so many freshmen that were failing back on the right track in such a short amount of time? Flipping. That's how.

Flipping, guts and determination.

I knew it was a great PR story, but that's not what got me so excited to share their experience with other educators. What got me so excited was me thinking 'this would have helped me so much when i was a student.'

I was never the strongest test taker and really struggled with Math and Science courses...to the point of tears because I just 'couldn't get it'. Like Troy's son- I felt like i understood the concepts in class, but once i got home, I couldn't remember anything.

Think of how many other students struggle with similar issues? College students, those returning to school after a period of time away from studying, international students, lifelong learners- its a model that can benefit everyone. This has the potential to really make a positive change in education!

...And no one else was 'flipping' on this scale.

I had to help get this example out in the public. If I was this inspired by Clintondale's experiment, just think how inspired other educators, students and parents could be!

The story is out there and flipping is gaining more and more traction with no signs of slowing down.

I have huge admiration for Greg, his staff and his students for taking a risk and trying something new under a huge amount of pressure.

This model of integrating technology into learning is changing the way education is delivered. And I am honored that I got to not only be a small part of helping to spread their story, but I'm also honored that I can now call Greg Green a good friend.

Rachael Parker
TechSmith Corporation

Taking calculated risks is not the norm within schools, however, where there is risk there is often great reward, and our school children deserved everything we have to give to them. If not us, then who else? With our intentional decision to flip, we now have become the school by which everyone is intrigued. We have been visited by over 300 educators from 12 different countries.

Watch Our Story
http://nationswell.com/michigan-clintondale-high-school-flipped-classroom-success/

I am not sure what we would have done, if we did not do something differently. How does one group expect to significantly change their outcome if they do not examine their entire purpose and process. What we have all learned as a staff and school is that we all have a passion to make wonderful achievements happen. We also have found that sometimes the most dedicated educators, with most difficult learning circumstances, can produce the most wonderful, amazing and heartfelt learning opportunities. Without a fabulous set of dedicated staff and patient students, this story would have been similar to other school failure stories. It is with great pride that, with everyone's persistence and willingness to change, we have successfully disrupted a school instructional structure that has been in place for 300 years. It was something that most people said could not and would not be done. Our goal was not to be in the history books but rather to find a way to afford our students and ourselves a chance to be successful. It has been an honor to serve our students and families, who needed us the most.

Through our work, we are hoping that we have found the core source of a school stakeholder's frustration, thus, reducing the tension in schools and ultimately giving students and teachers more control of their learning and teaching. We, as a staff, have uniquely discovered that school failure was not because we were not trying hard, but that our school routines were not aligned with the effort and support we had offered.

For the past three hundred years, schools have not changed that much. Teachers have been sharing what they know and students have been practicing at home. This routine has left many teachers, parents, and students frustrated. As a teaching staff, we felt that same frustration that many have day after day. It was in 2010 that we finally placed a stake in the ground and said we all have had enough.

What is most important is not the attention that we have received for flipping our classrooms in our entire school, but rather the importance our new model's impact has had on student learning and achievement . It is often hard to explain what it felt like to go through some difficult times; however, I have begun to realize that those hard times are now lessons from which others may learn. Those lessons were invaluable, and we feel honored to share them with educators across the globe.

There are several components to the flipped school and classroom that we must bring forward before we start. A flipped classroom instructional effectiveness only goes as far as our thoughtful and reflective professional practice takes us. The overall idea of a flipped classroom is to ensure that we have the time and the opportunity to fully support and implement what learning research reveals. It is still about great reflective teaching and learning practices. It is based on teaching and learning strategies that move student achievement. A teacher's daily classroom instructional routines and practices are still the keys to raising student achievement. Today's advanced technologies simply allow all of us to be more efficient and effective in our day to day processes.

Finally, we hope that this workbook allows to you to learn along with us and that all of our efforts have not been miscalculated, but rather lessons learned and our reflections upon them. May this workbook start your reflective learning process for you and your staff.

Best,

Greg Green, Principal and staff

Andy Scheel, Andy Kastl, Tom Fiori, Alex Taylor, Tracey Kasom, Rob Dameron, Janeen Denbaas, Mike Jones, Kelly Loria, Kristi Schneider, Jim Scarcelli, Chris George Malfroid, Dave Schindler, Jason Machalak, Julie Shier, Todd Swanboro, Mike Ward, Steve Moskal, Joe

Ferzo, Amy Merlo, Deb McNerlin, Erica Rudolph, Pat Laughlin, Chris Carpenter, Rob Townsend, Anita Anderlite, Mike Finn, Emily Pearcy, Nancy James, Renee Nota, Marci Dotson, Erik Glasius, Elizabeth Dalton, Jodie McGavin, Patrick Walters, Rick Filbey, Len Lewandowski, Dawn Sanchez, Meloney Cargill, .Kim Spriggs, Marci Glasius, and Kathy Zabel

Beginning Thoughts

Many schools, in order to fix themselves, have decided to purchase wireless Internet services as well as devices such as IPads and/or Chromebooks and some new learning applications. They have even gone as far as getting new furniture to change their school's learning problems. Yet, even with all the large investments, why do we as educators still feel a sense of frustration? We made all these changes and investments and still received the same learning outcomes - they were not the answers to our teachers' or students' success. As many experienced educators say in the teacher's lounge, "it is just the latest fad".

What we have discovered over the past five years is that just buying more tools, without an intentional learning and work purpose, is a big mistake. One sees it in schools today, when all students have IPads but teachers received no training on how to use them properly. We are so thankful that we had the opportunity to think outside the box and challenge ourselves to find the answers even if that meant starting over. We had to become very intentional about what we do and how we use the technology related tools we already had, and we had to do it without spending any more money.

Moving forward, as you reflect on our daily instructional routines and classroom practices you need to ask yourself what is your sole purpose as an educator? How do you generally use your classroom time? According to research, which of your teaching and learning strategies are the most important in regards to improving student achievement? And finally, which technologies align with your and your students' expectations, goals, and efforts?

The Bottom Line: Why Flip?

A flipped classroom is not a technology plan. It is simply a way to create a **learner-centered classroom** and intentionally use our current technologies to help us with the learning process.
It would seem that an effective learning delivery model for our classrooms should easily allow and encourage educators to be present in supporting our students during their active learning stages. In general, school research indicates that a *teacher*, in a supportive learning environment, can have the greatest and most positive effect on student learning.

Students need someone to show them, redirect them, and explain to them during the most crucial active learning times and activities how to learn what they need to know. They need someone to artfully put together learning activities that are well thought out and readily monitored, and even tweaked, based on their individual and the group's level of understanding. Counterintuitively, teachers send most practice activities home with students to work in a non-supportive learning environment.

Therefore, when deciding to flip your classroom, a teacher or even school makes an intentional decision to reshuffle the order of their classroom learning routines in order to better support the students during the active learning stage.

Initial Thoughts Regarding Our Core Foundations of Alignment

In the beginning of our flip process, we needed to examined how we were systematically built. We asked ourselves what was our purpose? Why were students coming to school, and what were we doing with them while they were seated in our classrooms?

After a year of observing 34 of our teachers' lessons, we found that 83% of our class time (55 minutes) was spent on telling students what they need to know and do while only 17% of our time was spent on actually applying a skill set. We began to ask ourselves, "is that the norm"?

In most of our classrooms, teachers had taken the majority of class time sharing and reviewing information in class, then students actively practice assigned learning activities at home - we hoped. This was logical because before the onset of the Internet in the mid 1990's, schools were thought of as the lone reliable source of academic related information. Before the 1990's, how else did we expect educators broadcast their messages to their students outside of class?

Prior to this technological shift, parents had been through school before and could help their student at home. Parents were somewhat equipped to handle the the learning activities because the classroom subjects, expert language, and the applications had not drastically changed since they went to school. Parents were connected to the classroom experience and they could help guide students through the homework process because they had been through it before.

Since 1983-84, there has been an increased sense and call for a new and more rigorous school curriculum. Each country, including the United States, has readily increased their schools' learning expectations for their students. Global leaders have recently challenged educators to push their students with faster processes and a more rigorous curriculum in order to meet the demands of a global and competitive environment.   As schools and students have built this fast track they forgot one thing, what about those people who help with the practice at home? Beginning with Everyday Math, students suddenly brought home learning activities and strategies that parents had never seen before. Prior to this increase in rigor, parents could support the academic lessons based on familiarity and recollection but now they could not. In fact, we had unintentionally left parents behind.

Fundamentally, as we shifted our K-12 students to a new and more rigorous workload, we forgot that parents need additional training to help assist in the explanation of the new homework. With a shift to a rigorous curriculum, the outside household can no longer support the learning process at home. It is an issue that is now front and center, staring directly at us.

With the recent economic downturn, schools and their personnel are being asked to do more with less. Thus, educating and supplying our parents and homes with additional community educational services and tools is unreasonable for most schools. Yet, there is a way. When we examined our schools from the outside looking in, we notice that they are set up with experts and resources that could be easily aligned with the learning activities as expected. Schools even have a wealth of support services that treat and support students who need help outside of their classroom. Given that parents or guardians cannot readily support the learning process, schools are essentially the only place that can. Therefore, it makes sense to explore a flipped classroom and even a flipped school model which naturally supports a learner with their expertise and school's existing resources.

Where Have We Seen Flip Before?

Flipping some learning routines to give learners immediate attention and feedback and thus giving a teacher or expert better control is nothing new. What is new is our new flip label and the attention we we are placing on it.

Here are some examples of flipped teaching. Remember, we simply flip our existing teacher subject review and student practice routines in order to make it more supportive for a student and more immediate for a teacher.

Athletic Coaches - If you have ever been around a bunch of athletic coaches for extended period of time, they are *control* freaks when it comes to their team. Thus, flipping their routines and spending the most time they can practicing with their players makes total sense to them. In most cases, coaches have players review simple plays in a playbook outside of their practice and then have them practice those plays right in front of them the next day. Coaches and players also use technologies such as video film to encourage collaboration and provide meaningful and immediate feedback.

Art and Foreign Language Teachers - Elective teachers are often realistic about what students can do at home. How can they expect parents to assist their student with the exercises of which they have no knowledge? If you closely examine how these teachers arrange their instructional routines, you will notice they do the majority of their work in class. What these teachers realize is that most students cannot duplicate their learning environment, supplies, technologies and expertise. Thus, they simply do it in class.

Everyone Else - What is really important when defining flip is that we DO NOT base our flip on using current day technologies. Technologies will continue to advance, so basing learning on something that is constantly changing is short-sighted. What we can build from: our expertise, research based learning, and teaching activities.

Bringing Others With You

All this may make sense to you and you feel motivated and are looking to change; however, there are many skeptics and naysayers. How do you bring them along, so they do not bring you down?

If you are an administrator or teacher leader, how do you convince a group of people to flip their classrooms? How can you show how reshuffling classroom routines will ultimately help people from burning out in the long run?

When talking about flipping a classroom, the conversation must be centered around the question, "what individual problems is the flipped classroom going to solve for each type of stakeholder?" Politically, we can all say it is for the children, but making personal changes to our daily routines is all about, "how am I going to benefit from changes?" Therefore, focusing on the benefits for a teacher or a school are paramount. Does a new system of delivering information reduce their workload redundancies? Does it allow them to share their expertise with their colleagues? Does it reduce teachers' frustrations with student homework and create better relationships among teachers' peers, colleagues, and other professionals? The answer is a resounding, yes!

Find the benefits in flipping for each one of the groups and then one will be able to craft your messaging according to who you are talking to:

- Teacher benefits
- School administrator benefits
- School district benefits
- Student benefits
- Parent benefits

 Craft a one page letter to whoever you audience is. Remember, it is all about the problems you solve for your specific audience.

How can you align your existing classroom routines, resources, expertise and expenditures to assist in the learning process? A little preparation on your end will help relieve some of the tensions that your students and staff might have with the current instructional process.

Examining What We Currently Do

What Support Resources Do You Currently Have and What Are You Going to Need?

First and foremost, the flip is not just simply a technology plan, but rather a change in process for which a school and/or classroom teacher properly aligns their current supports and resources to garner better learning control and create a more productive and efficient learner-centered classroom.

Most educators and professionals associate the flip teaching model strictly as a way to successfully implement technology. Yet, their support of their students' learning falls way short of what their students need. However, what is most important is that we align our process and delivery to the resources and expertise we have.

 First, write out or examine a typical opening lesson that you might do with your students to introduce a topic or unit.

 Next, make a list of what you currently use ie..technologies, supplies, books in your classroom and what your students may need while they are practicing during that particular lesson. When making your list, please indicate which items your students will have immediate access to in class and what they may not have when practicing their homework.

 Reflect for a moment. Do all of your students have a trained expert to assist them with any questions they may have on their homework assignment? If a student is absent or a student does not understand something at home, do they have a chance to talk to you or clarify some way when they are at home? Do they have the necessary supplies and technologies to continue the learning at home?

 Now, brainstorm some ideas how you can **guarantee** that all of your students can have immediate access to your expertise, supplies, all the needed educational technologies and devices. HINT: Where might those things be located?

In the next few pages, please spend a moment answering the following questions. These questions will assist you in organizing your thoughts about what actual expert resources you currently have and what you may have to seek out to offer your students.

Big Picture Overview: Questions to Ask Yourself

Do you most often feel that you are on an island all by yourself in your classroom? Many people do. Maybe, as a teacher, you are comfortable with most topics but need a little help on just a couple of items?

If you are a principal or lead teacher, how can you maximize your school's expertise that you already have? How can you assign and involve your experts in order have them work with content/projects and in roles that they most enjoy doing?

Lets see how many experts you have around you?

- How many content experts are there in your school?
- Are there any content experts who are really skilled or enjoy teaching certain units or projects?
- Are there any teachers and staff who enjoy talking in front of large groups?
- Are there any staff who like to work behind the scenes and organizing information?
- Are there any staff who love gadgets and technology?
- Do you have school leaders who develop classroom procedures?

Leadership / Teacher
Step Two: Reshuffling Your Instructional Practices

Communicating the Flip with your Students and their Families

Communication regarding the flip is very important because we want to be clear about our purpose behind it. What is important is that we place the initial emphasis on **helping students more** rather than the technologies we are going to use. Remember, you are talking to parents and students, so the focus of your communication should be the value it has for them and not you. Take a few moments and think about your messaging by answering the questions below:

How are you going to explain the flipped classroom to students and parents?

- Why are you flipping your classroom routines?
- What will students be doing at home and at school?
- Where can I find other examples of a flipped classroom?
- What does the learning research indicate about a learner centered rather than a teacher centered classroom?
- What problem does the flipped classroom solve for a parent and student?

Instructional Practices: Flipped Lesson Planning

Evaluate and align your daily and weekly instructional routines

Technology should not be the immediate focus of a flipped classroom or a flipped school. The technologies involved within a flipped classroom should act as tools that support the teaching and learning and makes it a much more efficient process.

When learning how to flip, it is vital that a teacher understands how much time he or she spends on each activity in class. It is also important to examine how much students actually do, and how much support we give them in a single classroom /learning period.

 In the next exercise, please take a lesson that you are familiar with, then fill out the chart below and indicate in five (5) minute increments what your normal classroom activities are as you introduce a lesson. Pay close attention to how much time you are spending working hand-in-hand with your students and allowing them to take more control of the activity. Are you at the center of the stage or are they?

Teacher Directed	Student Directed
5	
5	
5	
5	
5	
5	
5	
5	
5	
5	

Evaluate how you currently deliver content. When evaluating your current traditional lesson ask yourself the following questions:

- Are the majority of the activities teacher centered or learner centered during your lessons?
- How much time do you spend supporting your students' classroom practice?
- What percentage of time are your students active or passive during the lesson?
- Do your students have a chance to learn from their mistakes?
- Does your feedback ever loop back around?

Flipping Your First Learner Centered Lesson - 80/20

When creating a flipped lesson for the first time, a general ratio for how much time a student is actively engaged in the assigned learning activities and how much a teacher talks to the entire group during one classroom period is what is referred as 80/20. 80% of the time, a teacher wants to stand and deliver a lesson, while the student practices or applies new information in class 20% of the time, if at all. Now, rearrange the same lesson so that 20% of the time you are lecturing, demonstrating and controlling the activities and 80% of the time your students are actively working, applying, demonstrating, analyzing, creating understanding, and evaluating what they know. What you are attempting to do is keep your students working and your feedback and your analysis of their work immediate. Remember, flipping your lesson is about flipping the amount of support you are giving your students and NOT about the technology that we use doing it. All of us can flip our lessons without using any of today's technologies. All of us have begun to realize that there is no significant expert support for our current home practice activities, thus simply having them review relevant materials at home and doing the learning activity in front of you suddenly makes learning manageable and meaningful for everyone.

 Now Flip Your Same Lesson
- Pull out the major points of your lecture / direct instruction so when you lecture to your class, its a simple 5-6 minute review of basic material.
- Create an independent exercise which lasts 15-20% of the class time.
- Create a group / collaborative exercise that lasts 15-20% of the classroom time.
- Create a teacher 'check in' with your students as an individual, small or large group review 10% of classroom time.
- Create an assessment well before the end of the hour so students can correct any misconceptions and everyone can loop the objective(s) back to you.
- The goal is to get your classroom instructional practice routines to be 20% about you and 80% about your students' learning.

Advanced Lesson Analysis and Reflection

After designing your first flip lesson, what opportunities did your students have time to:

- Assess their own learning?
- Explain their understanding to the class, in small groups or a large group "take control of the marker"?
- Do advanced study/ work - extend their understanding?
- Slow down if they were confused?
- Collaborate with peers and experts?

 **For Those Who Need More Time to Lecture Content**

How can you incorporate a long lecture into your weekly plans and still achieve an 80/20 ratio? Hint! How could you use blocks of days or the week?

Monday   Tuesday   Wednesday   Thursday   Friday

I hope each of us realizes the flip is just slightly changing what we currently do. There are so many examples of this practice going on in schools today. It does not have to be complicated. It is about making our classrooms about our students' activity and understanding rather than just ours.

What is important is that each of us realizes that a teacher and school can flip their classroom(s) without using any technology. What is vital is that we make the best of the time that we have with our students. Making our classroom learner-centered rather than teacher centered.

Creating a Series of Flip Lessons

Now it is your turn to get amped up! Not every single class is going to be the same. Go ahead now and apply the 80/20 lesson format to each kind of lesson you or your group might do.

- Introductory Lesson
- Skill Building Lesson
- Station to Station Lesson
- Inquiry based Lesson
- Project based lesson

Analysis of Your New Flipped Lessons

Task

After formulating your five different lessons, please evaluate and analyze the following:

- Within each lesson, what percentage of your lesson was based on large group direct instruction?
- If using any types of technologies, were there learning and work objectives associated with each technology component? Were the technologies that have been selected based on today's learning research?
- How did you assess each student's learning? Did your expert feedback loop provide for immediate feedback or did it extend into the next class meeting time?
- At the end of the lesson, did your students leave knowing the most essential core learning principles of that unit?

Within your lesson, did your students have a chance to:

1. Assess their own learning

2. Explain their understanding to the class, in small groups or a large group "take control of the marker"

3. Do advanced study/ work - extend their understanding

4. Slow down if they were confused

5. Collaborate with peers and outside experts

The flipped classroom in action: the above photo reveals the teacher as monitor and assessor of student learning, students engaged with one another while applying knowledge of the concept, as well as a student engaged in her work individually. The teacher is able to move around the class and help students individually, in pairs, or again as a group if students are struggling with the concept. The reflective nature of the flipped class allows the teacher to observe if the instruction is successful, where any gaps may lie, and how and when to proceed with further material according to student need and achievement. This process aligns teaching and learning objectives while fostering student growth and understanding of the subject material. The students are fully engaged in the application of their learning in the flipped classroom.

Tip! Here are some lesson templates that we have developed and helped us with our flipped process.

Lesson Template: Skill Development

Looping activity   Time: 5 minutes

Teacher: Large Group (video)   Time: 5 minutes (10)
(Teacher can stop video periodically)

Student Guided Practice   Time: 5 minutes (15)

Teacher Large Group (Bring back)   Time: 2 minutes (17)

Student Guided Practice   Time: 5 minutes (22)

Teacher Large Group (Bring back)   Time: 2 minutes (24)

Student Guided Practice / Groups   Time: 10-15 minutes (39)
(Teacher walk around)

Teacher Large Group Clarification   Time: 5 minutes (44)
(Teacher have students list questions)

Looping activity   Time: 5 minutes (49)

Formative assessment   Time: 5 minutes (54)

Lesson Plan: Rotational/Stations (Students Rotating)

Looping activity   Time: 5 minutes   (5)

Large group review: Time: 5 -10 minutes (15)
(Video and teacher guided feedback; key points)

Teacher review directions: Time: 2 minutes (17)
(Review expectations for each station)

Station One: New Content / skill development: Time: 8-10 minutes (27)

Station Two: Group work   Time: 8 -10 minutes (37)
(Students have written directions and expectations)

Station Three: Teacher guided station   Time: 8-10 minutes (47)
(Working at a table with a group of students; check understanding)

Station Four: Looping activity   Time: 8-10 minutes (57)
(Basic skill development on a computer)

Lesson Template: Inquiry Based

Looping activity: Time - 5 min. (5)

Large group inquiry question   Time - 5-10 min (15)
(Teacher asks large group the question based around why
show a video on a scenario)

Teacher review   Time - 2 minutes (17)
(Clarify with large group)

Second large group inquiry question   Time - 5-10 minutes
(27)
(Teacher asks large group the question based around "why")

Teacher review   Time - 2 minutes (29)
(Clarify with large group)

Group activity with (2-4) students per group   Time - 15 minutes (44)
(Teacher reviews what students working agreements and outcomes)

Teacher based inquiry exercise
(Have students write questions on the board or use sticky notes)

Lesson Template: Project Based

Teacher reviews important rubric/outline/ looping points and timeline Time 5 minutes (5)
(Students should have rubric, outline and timeline) - Loop

Teacher walks room / students work on projects   Time - 15 minutes (20)
(Students should be working on one thing and then the next based on given outline)

Students check in with the teacher at a station   Time - 20 minutes (40)
(Check in needs be individual check in or group)

Teacher and students clarification exercise   Time - 10 minutes
(50)
(Teacher or students can post questions on the board)

Students create checklist summary of their progress   Time - 5 minutes
(Students check off where they are at in comparison to outline and rubric
and hand in)

Lesson Plan Template: Group Work

Gather in Large Group   5 minutes (5)
(Explain rubric, expectations, assign groups and member roles and key working agreements)

Collaboration Exercise   15 minutes (20)
(Teacher walks room and checks on progress)

Check In   5 minutes(25)
(Brief report out by group reporter)

Continue Collaboration Exercise   15 - 20 minutes (45)
(Teacher walks around to assist groups)

Report Out   5 minutes (50)
(Student groups report out findings and progress)

List Areas of Concern on the Board   5 minutes (55)
(Students place a question for class to review)

Working Well Together

Tip!

Collaborative Work

Whether one works in schools or not, the ability to work with others is crucial to a learner's development. When creating groups within a flipped classroom, it is vital to have your groupings well organized and your routines well thought out.

Important factors to consider before including group assignments within a flipped classroom are:

- Where does your assignment fit with the overall curriculum?
- What are the overall purpose of your group project and what the learning goals?
- Are the learning goals specific, clear, worthy, realistic, and achievable?
- Are the activities meaningful and is there sufficient time to finish?
- Is there a plan in place re: group's size and mix?
- Is your assignment aligned with students interests, strengths, and learning needs?
- What resources are needed for the activity?
- What are the learners' roles and responsibilities?
- How will decisions will be made in the group?
- How will the learners be evaluated?
- How is your room going to be set up to emphasize collaboration?
- How are you going to be keeping track of students' time on task?
- Have you used an online discussion board?
- How would you design your assignment using an online discussion board?

Step 3: Adopting New and Intentional Technologies within Your Classroom

After one has flipped their instructional routines, there are some intentional decisions to make about the types of technology one uses in a classroom setting. When adopting web services in a classroom, many get caught up in using an abundance of these services and leave the students and themselves stressed out because of their disconnectivity.

When deciding on what types of technologies, softwares and web services one should regularly incorporate in a classroom, a teacher and/or school should first identify how that particular technology helps achieve the desired instructional and learning objectives in a classroom. Most importantly, how will the proposed item enable their students to achieve the desired result? If so, then a teacher and their students are using the technology for the achieve purpose for which it was intended. This is particularly important when selecting a one-to-one device in schools. If one wants students to write a great deal more, it might be better to order a laptop device that has a keyboard. However, when teachers and students want to use web apps like The Khan Academy, a classroom may consider adopting a tablet. One single device does not fit all learning situations; therefore, like many individual users deciding on what their own personal device they will use, a school must identify what type of work will be done and what is its learning objective.

Research indicates that teachers have the greatest effect on student achievement; therefore, within a flipped school, an administrator/instructional leaders should introduce simple technologies that enable a teacher to have more time working with his or her students. Teachers should not be sitting at their desk clicking through numerous steps within a single platform. As a result, teachers will spend more time on their computer rather than working with their students. The technologies chosen should streamline teachers and organizational activities so that teachers can work directly with their students. Any technologies that have teachers sitting at their desk for more than 90 seconds is defeating a flipped school's overarching purpose. The technologies adopted should be ones that speed up the activities and provide immediate feedback.

Lastly, when working with today's technologies, it is best to work with general decision making frameworks such as learning and organizational objectives for selecting a device, app or specific program or software. Always keep in mind that the technologies are just the tools that we use today, but the purpose of why we use them rarely changes. Technologies change so rapidly; what is chosen today probably will not be around five years later.

Leadership/Administrative Staff Questions

 Tip For Introducing Technology to Staff
If you are a technology integration specialist or administrator responsible for implementing and introducing technologies, here is a tip. Start with the most user friendly technology and move forward from there.

Before implementing a piece of technology, it is vital to work through the reasons why you might use that particular technology over another. Generally speaking, what is that type of technology going to do for a student? How are they going to further their learning and understanding? What skills are they going to develop with the assistance and implementation of the technology?

 Answer the following questions about how your existing or proposed classroom instructional technologies are going to support student learning?

- What are your learning and organizational objectives for each grade level or department?
- What are the baseline professional skills one needs to survive using new technologies?
- Can your current building technologies support your flipped effort?
- Who does one turn to for immediate assistance with their technology?
- What additional software and equipment are teachers going to need?
- Does your software request align with your current and available technologies?

Keys When Deciding to Adopt Classroom and School Technologies

 Harvard, in their research, has stated many times that educators make the mistake of placing the technology first rather than establishing the purpose around the technology. When a group is trying to establish strategies for adopting new and current technologies in a learning environment, there are several components one might consider before deciding:

Step One: First, establish some concrete learning / skill development objectives when adopting and using classroom technologies. By learners using your specific prescribed technologies or tech related assignments, what skills are you aiming to develop? For example, Chromebooks are to used to develop research, typing, and writing skills. Google Drive will be used to develop collaboration and communication skills. Google Drive will also develop a learner's evaluation and creativity skills and also assist learners with organizational skills.

Step Two: Let us not forget that there are professionals involved with the technology integration, so what are the work objectives that are related to learner achievement? If teachers make the biggest impact on student learning, why are we giving them technologies, softwares and platforms that complex and have multiple steps. If teachers and experts need to work with students, then we need to adopt technologies that enable them to connect, collaborate, and even breath once in awhile!

Student Learning Objectives

 When thinking about using a piece of technology within your instructional routines, have you clearly identified the learning objective around it? In other words, how does this program or hard technology assist my students with their understanding and learning? Finally, does learning research support that assistance and end result of your lessons?

Answer the following questions regarding your technology implementation challenge: What learning skills are you trying to get students to develop like the one described and represented above? What do you want students to be able to do by using a web service or software?

For example, if using an online discussion board ie Google Groups, what do you want to provide for students during this collaborative environment?
- Do you want to provide students immediate feedback?
- Do you want to provide students better review opportunities?
- Encourage thought and dialogue and why is that important?

Do your thoughts align with learning research?
- For example, does learning research support a more collaborative environment?
- Does the proposed technology allow for more collaboration that is conducive to a classroom environment?
- Is it good to give students immediate feedback?
- Is it good to extend a student's thoughts and dialogue?

 Direct links to a person's skill-set and classroom activities allows for a smooth user transition. It provides a solid foundation from which to build the technology integration plan. Google created their Google Docs and Drive to look like Microsoft's Office so that a transition onto their platform would be easily done. If your students use a mobile device all the time, maybe teachers should push messages to them using services like Remind. If teachers have a busy professional and personal lifestyle, maybe administrators should only introduce technologies that enable them to move quickly in class.

Before you move forward you want to ask yourself a few more questions:

- Will there be a big learning curve when using it?
- Is there simple and familiar language, such as a post, text or tweet?
- Do students and teachers already communicate that way?
- If so, how is the the technology similar?
- Do all have access to it?
- Can you work quickly in and out of the online platform?
- Is it related to something you and your staff already do, such as hold classroom discussions?
- Do you have some work and communication rules already established?
- Will monitoring be easily done for immediate feedback?

If it is aligns well, it is probably a good idea to start moving forward.

Types of Technology Associated with the Flipped Classroom

Web Video
One piece of technology that can benefit teachers is web video. Services like YouTube are a great tool to use in our classrooms.
It can provide solutions for absent students and teachers, communicating consistent messaging, and making information more manageable.

 Web Video Tips
When using web video, it is important to remember some general guidelines when assigning web video for viewing:

- First, you don't have to make videos on fancy softwares. There are so many videos that are free to teachers, you would be surprised. Here are some helpful sites to get you started:
  - www.goorulearning.org
  - www.khanacademy.org
  - www.sophia.org
  - www.braingenie.com
  - www.teded.com

- Research indicates that in order to keep learner's attention, videos for high school students should be no more than six (6) minutes. The younger your students are, the shorter the video. There are some great 1-2 minute videos available online.
- Give students a reason to watch the videos. Assign a quiz or build an assignment around the video so that students watch it.
- Make sure the video can be seen on multiple devices such as phones and tablets. Each student will have their own personal device and we want to make sure they can watch it.
- Give students a couple of days to watch the video. No one likes surprises, and some students may not have access; therefore, giving them a chance to make the necessary arrangements is best.
- Lastly, try and get a partner teacher or expert to do some videos with you or find other web videos. The flipped classroom is collaborative setting for both a teacher and their students.

When Using Web Video Sites in Class - YouTube

 At this point, ask yourself the following questions about video?

- Can you flip your classroom routines so that they follow the 80/20 rule without using a web video?
- Do you have to create all the videos yourself or do you have someone else who could assist you?
- Can you take videos from another web source i.e. Khan Academy?
- Can you have your students do the web videos i.e. Math Train TV?
- What would be the easiest topic and subject with which you start?
- How are students going to view the videos?
- How are you going to post or send them i.e Blogger, Remind 101?

Creating a Web Video

In some cases, a teacher enjoys creating videos for their classroom or just cannot find the right instructional videos to use. Here are some helpful tips when recording a video to share with students. Many teachers and professionals use a powerful technology called a screen capture. There are some great softwares for creating screen capture video. It is best to start with simple screen capture software that allows a user to be in and out of its platform within three to five steps. Remember, one does not want to get caught up in the process but rather make the entire process easier and more convenient. It is best to start with something simple and progress to a more difficult and complex systems as one's confidence and efficiencies grow. Here are some companies that make screen capture software.

http://www.screencast-o-matic.com
http://www.techsmith.com

Storyboarding Your Video Ideas First!
When creating a screen capture video, it is a good idea to storyboard your video message. This technique allows you to transition well and seamlessly move through your content. This gives your learner a better overall viewing experience. If you are reviewing a concept or website from the Internet, an expert should consider tabbing the web pages, there is no delayed pausing when moving from one page to the next.

Storyboard Video	Standard		Topic	
	Unit		Teacher	

Topic:
Main points

Topic:
Main points

Topic:
Main points

Topic:
Main points

Topic:
Main points

Topic:
Main points

THINK! **Video Creation Questions for You**

- If you are deciding to record a video, what are you thinking about recording?
- If you are part of a group, who selects who is going to record what lesson? What criteria are they going to use?
- When are the experts suppose to record video content?
- Are outsiders suppose to be able to view the videos? Are they password protected?
- How are people going to share the videos within the school, department, classroom? Blogs, LMS, or text messages.

- How is a video and a staff's digital flipped content going to be approved for public viewing?
- Who is evaluating the video content? Who is going to change the content?

 Online Discussion Boards

One of the most effective ways for doing collaborative work is posting to a discussion board i.e. Google Groups. These online discussion forum boards allow a teacher and other students to contribute to the conversation using an online comment stream.

Assessment Technologies

A flipped classroom, like any classroom, should contain an assessment of the lesson and the learning for that day. There are assessment tools that allow for quick and easy diagnostic feedback. What is most important is that there is continuous feedback for both the learner and the teacher. This enables a teacher and students to quickly adapt based on the immediate results that day. What had also realize that these assessments should be given so that students have a chance to make the necessary corrections before they leave.

- Online polling ie.. www.polleverywhere.com
- Online grading with webcam www.gradecam.com

 Sharing Information with Your Students; Texting, Blogging and Learning Management Systems

When a teacher begins to post materials online, they soon realize that it would be nice to post something once and not have to repost it. Using a learning management system is generally for advanced technology users. Some simple ways to share information with students are messaging them assignments using Remind or Celly. Teachers can simply find a video or post a video on YouTube and then share the link with their students. If a teacher would like to post notes and keep a series of posts, then a blog may satisfy their quest, such as Edublog, Blogger and Wordpress. For those experienced posters a service like Edmodo or Eduongo and Moodle may meet your needs. These services contain all in one systems that connect calendars, gradebooks, collaboration and content organizational tools.

Step Four: Sustainability

 Streamline and Automated Technologies

One of lessons most learned is how many challenges we have taken on and the exhausting processes with which we are engaged. Classrooms are a very, very busy place with lots and lots of interruptions. What is sensible is to select technologies that enables a teacher to automate things and skip steps in the communication process and feedback process.   All in all, we have asked all of educators to do more and more with less and now it is time to simplify the process.

Physical Classroom Space Design

Once one flips a classroom or session, it becomes readily apparent how important a learning space's physical design contributes to the outcome of the lesson. The key in a flipped learning classroom or session is making sure the physical classroom contributes positively to the activities that you are performing. When leading a lesson one wants to ensure that physical set-up does not hinder your ability to differentiate your lesson and support your students.

THINK! Where do you hold your learning activities in your classroom? If you are going to differentiate your instruction, the type of space will you need to best support what you asking students to accomplish is important.

- Where are the students going to listen and take part in large group exercises?
- What is the set up for collaborative exercises so students can work with one another? Can the furniture be easily moved?
- If you were going to work with students, how can you do so in a manageable way?
- When working in collaborative groups, how does one display their idea?
- How can one set up their room in order to take part in following modes of instruction during one classroom / learning period:

- Large group
- Small group
- Teacher guided
- Independent
- Skill building

Go ahead and draw out your classroom.

Draw Out Your Classroom

Does your space allow you to move in and out of the student work areas?
Does your space allow your students to collaborate with one another?
Does your space have a place where students can build independent skills?
Does your space allow you to have a teacher check in station?

Flip is a Reflective Teaching and Learning Process

 As professionals, we always want to evaluate our work. Here is a helpful reflection sheet to begin the process.

Instructional Reflections for Staff

The flip teaching is about being learner centered in class under our 80/20 lesson format. Do you find it easy or difficult to stay within those parameters when developing your lessons? Why?

Explain how your space design prohibits or encourages instructional strategy implementation? Why? What would you do differently?

Do you use discussion boards on a daily or even monthly basis? Why or why not?

List two to three (2-3) instructional strategies that you use on a regular basis. Why do you use them? What would encourage you to use a bigger variety or do you feel that 2-3 are enough?

Based on the learning goals that you set at the beginning of the year, what does your data reveal? What instructional or planning adjustments, if any, would you make?

Explain how you regularly assess students within your daily lesson. If a monitor came in, could you provide immediate evidence? If so, through by what means ie.. sample student work, formative assessment strategy, pictures, or other means?

If you were to explain the biggest instructional hurdle that only deals with your professional transformation, what would that be and why?

How has your role as a teacher changed by not having to lecture for the majority of the hour?

Do you feel like you have more or less control over the amount of work that students do by flipping your classroom? If so, why or why not?

Reflecting back three to four years ago in what ways are your instructional practices and routines more student focused?

Explain how you could provide evidence that shows that you have instructionally transferred the learning ownership from you to your students?

List all the technology platforms that you currently use and why.

Flipped Instructional Observations for an Instructional Team Leader and/or Administration

 As teachers reflect on their own flip instruction, administrative staff can support the flip by using our classroom walk-through and unofficial observation checklist.

Classroom Walk-through

Observation Date:

Observation Time:

Check the **dominant activity** and the time spent on each.

_____ Large group and how much time spent _____mins.

_____Small group _____mins.

_____Individual work _____mins.

_____Warm up _____mins.

_____Watching multimedia_____mins.

_____Taking an assessment _____mins.

_____Individual activity _____mins.

What levels of Bloom's Learning Taxonomy did the lesson appear to reach?

Please circle each one once it is observed.

Remember - Understand - Application - Analysis - Evaluation - Creation

Noteworthy instructional practice observations

Please place an "x" next to the following after you observe it:

_____Connects with prior learning

_____ Has students use quality questioning techniques

_____ Is modeling for students the desired objective or outcome

_____Students are actively participating _____percentage of students participating

_____Regularly checks for understanding _____uses technology to display learning data

_____Feedback loop in immediate during learning assessments

_____ A variety of learning modes and opportunities

_____Critical analysis activities appear to be clearly articulated

_____Learning strategies and techniques for the students modeled and well-thought out

_____Personal reflection by students

_____Reflective writing exercise

Classroom Procedures / Space Design

Please place a "X" when observed during a lesson.

_____ Classroom rules and policies are visibly apparent to all students

_____ Classroom routines are extremely well scripted out

_____ A classroom's physical space and design clearly encourages ideal behaviors

_____A classroom's furniture arrangement clearly encourages differentiation

_____The classroom set up encourages a collaborative learning group

Lesson Objectives / Curriculum Objectives

_____Learning objective/goal is prominently displayed in the room

_____ Objective(s) is/are part of the critically identified curriculum group

_____ There is evidence that the critical objectives are being spiraled or looped

_____ Objective(s) is/are reviewed and referenced by the teacher

_____ Objective (s) is/are also articulated well by the students when asked

_____ Objective(s) appear to be connected with curriculum content and with strategy

_____ End objectives (s) is/are clearly centered around the development of one's skill set

_____ Classroom objective (s) is/are aligned with curriculum and standards

Materials

_____ On-line materials are visible, current and available to <u>all</u> stakeholders

_____ On-line materials are well organized and presented in a logical manner

_____ A teacher's web address is posted and visible in class

_____ On-line materials are current and follow the curriculum expectations

_____ Classroom materials are at the proper reading and grade level

_____ Classroom materials provided clear direction for student engagement.

_____ Classroom materials appear to have met the expected rigor and relevance

_____ Classroom materials have been presented in a logical fashion

_____ Homework is a continuation of an in-class assignment

_____ Directions regarding outside support are apparent and regularly communicated

Video Use

_____Video was presented <u>before</u> learning session began

_____Video was visible on a website / blog

_____Videos were pushed out to the students through an electronic delivery system ie Twitter

_____ Instructor created a video themselves

_____Instructor used another expert's video that met the curriculum expectations

_____Instructor used a student created video so to promote personalization

_____Instructor used a community led video

_____Web video was not used nor readily available to students

_____Not applicable

Collaboration Exercises / Discussion Board

_____Group work is visibly apparent on a virtual discussion board / classroom exercise

_____Key working agreements are visible and directions are clearly communicated

_____Reporting out procedures are in place before the activity begins

_____Each group member has a specific job and it is part of a teacher's evaluation rubric

_____The assignment is clearly related to the content expectations

_____ The assignment is related to the development of a student's skill and/or learning strategy

_____The prescribed assignment uses all the participants skill sets

_____The prescribed assignment enables students to tap into another's learning foundation

_____The prescribed assignment allows for instructional monitoring and immediate feedback

Data Collection

_____Data was collected immediately for critical instructional adjustments and documentation

_____Students analyze learning data in order to promote individual and classroom ownership

_____Learning data is displayed for a student's and parent's quick reference

_____Learning data is reasonably displayed and can be regularly shared with stakeholders

_____Department wide data is available to be shared with internal collaborators

Check Teacher Activity Level with the Students - Observed

_____ Minimal (Walked around)

_____ Average (Walked around and answered a few questions)

_____ Very good (Walked around, engaged every student, answered questions,

    and demonstrated for students)

_____ Excellent (Walked around, asked a few questions, answered questions, demonstrated for students, and checked for individual understanding and had an immediate feedback loop)

What did you observe about 80/20?

How did the teacher and student spend their time? Indicate how a teacher spent their time during your classroom observation. Indicate on the timeline below whether it was a teacher led or student led activity.

5 minutes:

10 minutes:

15 minutes:

20 minutes:

25 minutes:

30 minutes:

35 minutes:

40 minutes:

45 minutes:

50 minutes:

55 minutes:

60 minutes:

Instructional Strategies Observed

Place the amount of time (mins.) a student working with the following instructional strategies or an "x" when appropriate.

_____ Graphic Organizer / Organizational

_____ Cues / Questions - Inquiry Based

_____ Decision maker

_____ Investigation

_____ Problem Solving

_____ Analysis

_____ Application

_____ Compare / Contrast

_____ Classification

_____ Physical Model

_____ Practice

_____ Providing Feedback

_____ Summarizing

_____ It was visibly apparent that the learning strategies selected by the lead learner clearly align with the skill that is being developed

Based on your observations, how much time was spent students practicing?

What percentage did the teacher take control of the classroom activities?

Please list the top (3) strategies and their time spent on each one from your lists above.

1.

2.

3.

_____Was a timing device was used by the teacher in order to keep good track of time.

General Notes:

_____

_____

_____

_____

_____

_____

Areas of Strength:

_____

_____

_____

_____

_____

Areas of Suggested Improvement:

_____

_____

_____

_____

_____

Observer: _____**Date:**_____

Additional notes and attachments:

Good Luck!

I hope that you found the flipped process as beneficial as we did. Here is story of one of our students for whom we made the difference.

Video   http://t.co/AoOsEDKmsA

We hope our flipped learning tips helped you get started in the flipped learning process. These thoughts and methods helped us changed the lives of our students and us as educators. If you have any questions or would like to visit us, please feel free to contact us at:

Clintondale High School
35200 Little Mack
Clinton Township, MI 48035
734-945-3464
greeng@flippedhighschool.com

71429661R00027

Made in the USA
Lexington, KY
20 November 2017